La Famiglia Ricette:
An Italian
Culinary Travel Cookbook
By
T.R. Threston

Notting Hill Publishing

Notting Hill Publishing

103 New Oxford Street, London

ISBN-13: 978-0692306673
ISBN-10: 0692306676

Notting Hill Publishing, London, UK © 2014

1

Dedicated to my Grandmother "Jennie" & Italian food lovers everywhere.

Notting Hill Publishing, London, UK © 2014

About The Author

T.R. Threston

Notting Hill Publishing, London, UK © 2014

T.R. Threston is the C.E.O. of World Guide Publishing©, and, a well-known, and, highly respected, award winning luxury travel writer. She worked as a travel agent for a number of years before turning to a career in writing for magazines, newspapers, online media, and, guidebooks.

In addition to her work, T.R. Threston serves on the Board of Trustees of "The New York Social Network", a charitable organization that helps raise awareness & funds for non-profit organizations. She also served as Chairwoman of "New York Travel Writers Society" 2013/2014, and, is actively involved with "Collective Changes" (a non-profit women's economic empowerment organization) where she serves as a Global Ambassador.

T.R. Threston also leads a KIVA team (KIVA makes mirco-loans in increments of $25 to entrepreneurs and students in over 70 countries,) and, Threston is also involved with several United Nations non-profit organizations including Giving Tuesday where she serves as a Social Media Ambassador, and, she is also a Messenger of Humanity where she helps to spread awareness about the United Nations program "World Humanitarian Day." She is a member of the 2013 Women's Museum Honor Roll, and, supports a number of charities on the local level.

Notting Hill Publishing, London, UK © 2014

Introduction

I am not a professional chef. However, I am someone who is passionate about Italian food and Italian cooking. And, don't let the surname "Threston" throw you, I promise you there is plenty of Italian and Sicilian blood coursing through my veins to justify my attempt at an Italian cookbook. So how did I get here? Like most journeys, it is a long story, so, I'm giving the abbreviated version of my adventures in culinary writing. I've been a travel writer, and, more recently a publisher of travel magazines, articles, and, books; and, I've always enjoyed food, and, decided to jump on the culinary travel band-wagon.

Notting Hill Publishing, London, UK © 2014

In Fall, 2014, I launched a magazine called "The Road Less Eaten", and, it brings together the latest trend of culinary travel and vacations. In layman's terms it simply means that people are taking vacations (holidays) that involve or revolve around food – be it cooking lessons or simply eating delicious foods in destinations worldwide, and, from the looks of things this trend isn't going to go away any time soon. This book, while primarily a cookbook, also offers travel tips and suggestions throughout Italy, based on my own experiences. And, I must humbly thank my good friend, award winning travel and fashion photographer Robert Bonhomme, for the absolutely stunning photographs he (except where noted) provided for this book.

And, the majority of credit for the recipes in this book go to my Grandmother affectionately known as "Jennie". Oh sure, my Mother and I have "tweaked" her recipes over the years, but, I have to give credit where credit is due. What makes this story a bit more unique than most is that my Grandmother lost both her parents, and, was living in an orphanage in Sicily by four years of age. I'm not sure who taught her to cook or if somehow it just came naturally to her; regardless, she turned out to be an incredible cook, and, since I have no children of my own, I wanted to do something to make sure her recipes live on which brings us back to here and now.

I was approached to write this book by Elizabeth Brown, who is the C.E.O. of Notting Hill Publishing, after she attended a dinner party in London where she met mutual friends, and, as the saying goes "The rest is history." It is my hope that you find these recipes easy to follow and that your results are as good as if I was in the kitchen cooking for you.

So with no further adieu, I present to you "La Famiglia Ricette" or "My Family Recipes." Buon appetito!

Notting Hill Publishing, London, UK © 2014

Italy/Italia

One of the best descriptions I ever heard of Italy was someone described it as a drug. (Meaning once is never enough, and, it is so addictive that you'll want to return time and time again.) And, there has to be a grain of truth in there someplace because Italy consistently rates in the top when it comes to the most visited countries in the world.

In this book I will be sharing my family recipes, and, also Italy itself, and, including some of it's most popular regions to visit: Rome, Venice, Florence/Pisa/Tuscany, Naples, and, Sicily. And, whether you've never been to Italy or you consider it your home away from home, you'll come to learn that Italy has much to share with the world beyond fabulous cuisine.

Notting Hill Publishing, London, UK © 2014

Italy is located in Southern Europe and it forms a boot shaped peninsula; and, it also encompasses the islands of Sicily and Sardinia. Each region of Italy is different, and, even the Italian language varies by dialect throughout the country.

Italy is rich in history and is a very ancient civilization. Evidence shows that human beings have been in the region for over 1.5 million years as evidenced by the tools found at Pirro Nord (located in the province of Foggia.) And, it has been concluded that <u>anatomically modern humans</u> (also known as anatomically modern Homo sapiens) lived in the region (known today as Italy) over 43, 000 years ago.

Modern Italy, as we know it today was formed on March 17, 1861. It survived two World Wars, and, today welcomes over 45 million visitors from around the world each year. Benvenuti in Italia! (Welcome to Italy!)

Notting Hill Publishing, London, UK © 2014

Rome

Rome is a dynamic, energetic city that gives New York a run for its money, and, traffic (not to mention getting across the street) is legendary in this ancient city. The first time visitor will (more than likely) be a bit hesitant to temp fate (as the locals do) by simply crossing a street when and where they so desire. It sounds crazy, but, that's life in Rome! (And, don't knock it until you try it!)

Sightseeing

There are many things to see and do in Rome, and, of course a few of the "must sees" include the Coliseum, the Forum, the Pantheon, and, the Vatican. Of course, the Vatican isn't really part of Rome, in fact, it isn't part of Italy. It is own country encompassed by the city of Rome.

During high season, lines at the Vatican are exceptionally long, and, can be avoided by booking your visit through a tour group that specifically expresses that you will "skip" the line or if you detest structured tours, try to get there in the afternoon.

Food

In Rome, Spaghetti Carbonara is king (see page 60 for recipe!) And, you'll find every variety imaginable in the Eternal City.

Notting Hill Publishing, London, UK © 2014
Photos by Robert Bonhomme

Sicily

In the past 15 or 20 years, Sicily has begun to come into it's own as vacation destination; and, with beautiful beaches, a unique and rich culture all it's own, and, some of the most popular Italian cuisine around it's hard to believe Sicily was overlooked for so long.

Sightseeing

While visiting Sicily be sure to see the UNESCO World Heritage sites of Valley of the Temples and Villa Romana del Casale. The Valley of the Temples (or Valle dei Templi – as it is known locally) is located in Agrigento, Sicily, and, is a significant archaeological site offering outstanding examples of Greek art and architecture. Villa Romana del Casale offers one of the largest, richest, and, most complex collection of Roman mosaics in the world. It dates back to the 4th Century, and, more than likely was a large farm or estate (known as a latifundium in Latin.)

Food

Sicily has made marvelous contributions to the word in terms of food. Try arancini which are rice balls stuffed with cheese (although sometimes meat) and fried to a golden brown -- see recipe page 37. Cannoli are another delicious contribution the Sicilians gave to the world – see recipe page 84. The ricotta cheese stuffed pastries are sweetened with powered sugar, and, are the perfect ending to any meal or great on their own as a snack. Ever have an Italian ice? It is based on Granita. And, you can thank the residents of Sicily for this tasty summer treat – see recipe page 87.

Notting Hill Publishing, London, UK © 2014

Sicily, Italy/Photo by Robert Bonhomme

Sicily, Italy/Photo by Robert Bonhomme

Napoli/Naples

Naples, Italy with Mount Vesuvius/Photo by Robert Bonhomme

Naples (or Napoli as it is known) has long suffered from a bad reputation, some jokingly refer to it as the Newark (New Jersey) of Italy. Having been born in Newark, NJ, I have a special empathy towards Naples. However, there is no denying Naples does have its share of problems. Problems that plague any big city, just about anywhere in the world. And, if you find yourself in Italy, and, are tempted to skip Naples altogether, keep in mind you're passing by the birth place of pizza among other treasures.

Yes! Naples is home to (nearly) everyone's favorite "junk" food. Pizza! And, the actual "birth" of pizza traces all the way back to 997 AD to the town of Gaeta which is roughly 1.5 hours north of Naples. Additionally, Naples services as a great jumping off point to explore Mount Vesuvius, Pompeii and Herculaneum, and it is the start one of the best coastal drives anywhere in the world: The Amalfi coast!

Notting Hill Publishing, London, UK © 2014

13

Venice

Without doubt, Venice is one of the most recognizable cities in the world. This "floating" city, located in Northeast Italy, was home to the legendary Giacomo Casanova (not to mention a number of Doges – some good, some not so much. And, numerous artists including Titian.)

Sightseeing

Venice (the entire city) is a UNESCO World Heritage Site, and, there is much to see, do, and, explore in this city of canals, bridges, and, dead-end foot paths and walkways.

Food

One of the most famous drinks in the world was created in Venice, Italy -- The Bellini it is made with sparking white wine (Prosecco) and pureed white peaches. Delicious anytime of year, and, especially refreshing in the summer months. Don't leave Venice without sampling this creation where it was born! Harry's Bar is located at Calle Vallaresso 1323, Venice, Italy and is owned by Cipriani S.A.

Gondolas

Gondolas are more for tourists than for locals, but, don't dismiss this mode of transportation simply because it is the touristy thing to do. Gondolas can snake through the smaller canals where water taxis cannot fit, and, many gondoliers are excellent tour guides. *Note: It is highly recommended that you negotiate both the rate and the length of the ride with the gondolier before you get into the boat.*

Notting Hill Publishing, London, UK © 2014

15

Florence/Pisa/

Tuscany

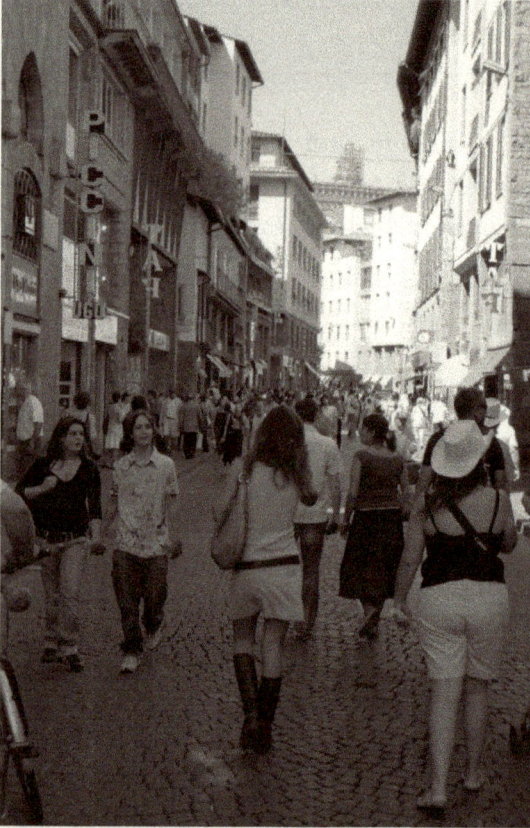

Florence, Pisa, and, Tuscany are on many travelers "must do" or "bucket lists" and with good reason. These are some of the most beautiful areas of Italy, and, it is world renounced for their vineyards and wines.

Sightseeing

Each hill town in Tuscany begins to blend into each other after a while, so, it is important to pick and choose your destinations; however, sometimes getting off your planned itinerary leads to the very best experiences while traveling, so, if something grabs your attention, and, you aren't on a tight schedule – go with the flow and explore! Enjoy!

If you are in Florence/Pisa and Tuscany mainly for the vineyards and wineries, it is recommended that you contact the facilities of interest directly. Some facilities, like their American cousins in Napa and

Sonoma valleys in California, are open to the general public, and, others are by appointment only or not open to the public at all.

Food

As you head North in Italy, pasta becomes less common and polenta and beans become the starchy favorite to many meals. Additionally, you'll encounter less fish, and, more meats including the famous Bistecca Alla Fiorentina (Florentine Steak.)

Abruzzo, Italy © Robert Bonhomme

Florence, Italy

Agriturismos
Agri What?

If you haven't hear of Italy's Agriturismos or know what it even means, you aren't alone. However, agriturismos are a great way to combine food and culture into one. Simply put -- an Agriturismo is a bed and breakfast, and, they range from one star to five stars just like any other resort, hotel or B & B.

*Agriturismo*s in Italy

The following agriturismos have at least a four star rating, and, have been assessed as such through visitor reviewed based websites. Contact information and amenities are listed. Prices are omitted due to the changing nature of time of year and demand. The listings are neither paid advertising nor endorsements of the agriturismos, rather they are an easy list to allow you to explore the different host agriturismos to help you select the one that may be best for you and your culinary travel needs in Italy or at least help get you started with your own plans. *(Please note this is a not a full list.)*

Agriturismo Antico Casale
Via Cermenna, 45, 80063 Piano di Sorrento Napoli, Italy Phone: +39 081 808 3462

Agriturismo Poggiacolle Farmhouse

Address: Strada di Montauto, 58, 53037 San Gimignano Siena, Italy

Phone:+39 0577 941537

Region: Tuscany

Agriturismo Poggiacolle offers views of mediaeval towers of San Gimignano, 2 km away (just under a 10 minute walk.) The property offers a panoramic swimming pool, and rustic accommodation decorated in a Tuscan country style.

Notting Hill Publishing, London, UK © 2014

Agriturismo Poggiacolle Farmhouse located in *San Gimignano Siena, Italy*

Amenities

- *Internet Free: WiFi is available in public areas and is free of charge.*
- *Outdoor: BBQ Facilities, Outdoor Pool, Grounds*
- *Activities Ping-Pong, Cycling, Bikes Available (free)*
- *Parking Free! Free private parking is available on site (reservation is not needed).*
- *Non-smoking Rooms*
- *Heating*
- *Languages spoken Italian, English*

Phone: +39 0577 941537

Email: info@poggiacolle.com

Agriturismo Marciano

Address: Strada della Befana, 5, 53100 Siena, Italy

Phone:+39 0577 47737

Region: Tuscany

Siena, Italy by Robert Bonhomme

Agriturismo Marciano is located near the walls of the Middle Age town of Siena in the heart of Tuscany.

Notting Hill Publishing, London, UK © 2014

Agriturismo Marciano, Siena, Italy

Amenities

- *Restaurant*
- *Pets allowed*
- *Typical products on sale*
- *Bike rental*
- *Credit cards welcome*
- *Air conditioning*

Phone: +39 0577 47737

Email: staff@agriturismomarciano.it

Notting Hill Publishing, London, UK © 2014

Agriturismo La Muratella

Address: Via Portuense, 1118, 00148 Roma, Italy

Phone:+39 0665 000012

Region: Rome/Lazio

Trevi Fountain, Rome, Italy

Agriturismo La Muratella, Rome, Italy

Located on the outskirts of Rome, and, is surrounded by olive groves and vineyards.

Amenities

- *Air conditioning*
- *BBQ facilities*
- *Facilities for disabled guests*
- *Family rooms*
- *Free parking*
- *Garden*
- *Heating*
- *Lift/Elevator*
- *Luggage storage*
- *Non-smoking rooms*
- *On-site parking*
- *Pets allowed*
- *Private parking*

Phone: +39 0665 000012   **Email:** info@agriturismomuratella.com

Agriturismo Podere Prasiano

Address: Via Frignanese, 5284, 41054 Marano Sul Panaro Modena, Italy

Phone:+39 059 596 6795

Region: Emilia-Romagna/Bologna

Modena, Italy

Located about 1 hour from Bologna in the Emilia-Romagna region offers a rustic setting in a working orchard.

Notting Hill Publishing, London, UK © 2014

Agriturismo Podere Prasiano, Modena, Italy

- *Amenities:*
- *Beverage Selection*
- *Free Breakfast*
- *Free High Speed Internet (WiFi)*
- *Free Parking*
- *Restaurant*
- *Swimming Pool*
- *Wheelchair access*

Phone: +39 0595 966795

Email: info@podereprasiano.it

Notting Hill Publishing, London, UK © 2014

Drinks, Antipasti & Appetizers

Notting Hill Publishing, London, UK © 2014

Limoncello

- 12 Meyer or Amalfi Lemons
- 1 lime - optional
- 2 (750 ml) bottles 100% proof vodka, divided
- 2 cups water
- 2 cups granulated sugar

Instructions

Remove yellow part of lemon peel either with micro-plane or sharp peeler. If any pith remains on the back of a strip of peel, scrape it off. (The pith is the white part of the skin, it is bitter.)

Place peels in an airtight glass jar and add one of the bottles of vodka. Seal closed (air tight) and place in dark location for 6 weeks to blend and ferment.

After 6 weeks, combine sugar and water in a small saucepan, bring to a boil over medium heat, stirring frequently, until the sugar has dissolved. This makes Simple Syrup. Allow the syrup to cool to room temperature.

Using sieve or several layers of cheese-cloth, strain the vodka from the peels and mix it with the remaining bottle of vodka and the syrup. Put the liqueur in bottles, seal tightly (cork or screw-top lid) and let the components marry, in a dark place, for at least 15 days before serving.

For drinking straight, store the Limoncello in the freezer.

Bruschetta

Bruschetta is always a crowd pleaser, and, it is one of the easiest recipes in the world. Even the novice cook will be able to make this tasty treat!

Ingredients

4 tablespoons olive oil
5 cloves garlic, finely minced
6 to 8 medium to large vine ripped tomatoes, chopped
1 tablespoon balsamic vinegar
16 whole fresh basil leaves, chopped or ripped into small pieces
Salt and freshly ground black pepper
1 whole baguette or crusty loaf of bread
1 stick butter

Directions

In a small plan, heat the olive oil over medium-high heat. Add the garlic and stir, lightly frying for about a minute, until translucent. (Browning makes garlic bitter, so do NOT brown.) Pour the garlic and oil into a mixing bowl and allow to cool slightly.

Add the chopped tomatoes, balsamic vinegar and basil to the bowl. Sprinkle lightly with salt and pepper. Toss to mix and coat, and then taste and add more basil if needed, then adjust salt and pepper to taste. Cover and refrigerate for at least two hours.

Cut the baguette into rolls on a diagonal. Melt 4 tablespoons of the butter in a fry pan and toast the bread on both sides until golden brown on both sides. Do not allow to burn. Set aside until ready to assemble.

Do NOT put the tomato mixture on the bread until you are actually ready to serve it. Otherwise, the bread will be soggy, and, you'll have a mess.

Notting Hill Publishing, London, UK © 2014

31

Fried Mozzarella Sticks

Ever tried to fry mozzarella sticks like the restaurants serve only to have the mozzarella ooze out and create a huge mess, and, you spent hours trying to clean your pan or deep fryer? The secret? Freeze the cheese!

Ingredients

1 1/2 cups Italian-style dried breadcrumbs
1 1/3 cups freshly grated Parmesan (Parmigiano Reggiano is best if you have it)
1 teaspoon salt
2 (16-ounce) blocks pasteurized mozzarella cut into long strips (about 4 in x 2in)
4 large eggs, beaten/whisked to blend thoroughly
1 1/2 cups olive oil
4 cups Marinara Sauce, recipe see page

Directions

Begin by cutting up your mozzarella. If you're in a hurry, you can also use pre-made string cheese mozzarella sticks from the grocery store.

In a medium to large bowl stir the bread crumbs, 1 cup of Parmesan and 1 teaspoon of salt together. Dip the mozzarella sticks/strips in the eggs to coat. Then immediately dip the sticks into the bread crumb mixture and roll to coat completely. Place the cheese sticks on a baking sheet. Repeat this process for each stick/strip until each has two coatings. Cover with plastic wrap and freeze until frozen.

**It takes about 2 to 3 hours for the sticks/strips to freeze

Preparing: Heat the oil in a large frying pan over medium heat. Working in batches, fry the cheese until golden brown, about 1 minute per side. Transfer the fried cheese to plates. Serve with the Marinara Sauce.

Marinara Sauce:

1/2 cup extra-virgin olive oil
2 small onions, finely chopped
2 garlic cloves, finely chopped
1/2 teaspoon sea salt, plus more to taste
1/2 teaspoon freshly ground black pepper, plus more to taste
2 (32 ounce) cans whole tomatoes
1 teaspoon, pre-mixed Italian seasoning (found in the spice aisle of your supermarket)

Directions:

Open the cans of tomatoes, and, crush using a potato masher or place in a blender for smoother sauce.

In a large pot, heat the oil over a medium-high flame. Add the onions and garlic and saute until the onions are translucent, about 10 minutes. Add salt and pepper. Add the tomatoes and Italian seasoning, and simmer uncovered over low heat about 1 hour. Season the sauce with more salt and pepper to taste.

Notting Hill Publishing, London, UK © 2014

Fried Zucchini Blossoms

It may sound strange at first, but, don't knock 'em until you try 'em!

Ingredients

1 cup all-purpose flour
1 cup sparkling water (still water will not work in this batter)
3/4 teaspoon salt, plus extra for seasoning
1/2 cup mozzarella cheese (grated)
1 green onion, finely chopped
Freshly ground black pepper
8 zucchini blossoms*
Vegetable oil, for frying

Note: Zucchini blossoms can usually be found at farmer's markets and specialty grocery store in major cities in the United States.

Directions

In a medium bowl, mix together the flour, water and salt until smooth. Set aside. (This is your batter for the flowers.)

Spoon 1 1/2 to 2 teaspoons of mozzarella cheese into each blossom. Close the blossoms and gently twist the petals to seal.

In a large heavy-bottomed saucepan, pour enough oil to fill the pan about a third of the way. Heat over medium heat until a deep-frying thermometer inserted in the oil reaches 350 degrees F.

Dip the stuffed zucchini blossoms in the batter and allow any excess batter to drip off. Fry for 1 to 2 minutes, turning occasionally, until golden brown. Allow the cooked blossoms to drain on paper towels.

Season with salt and serve with your favorite marinara sauce (if so desired)

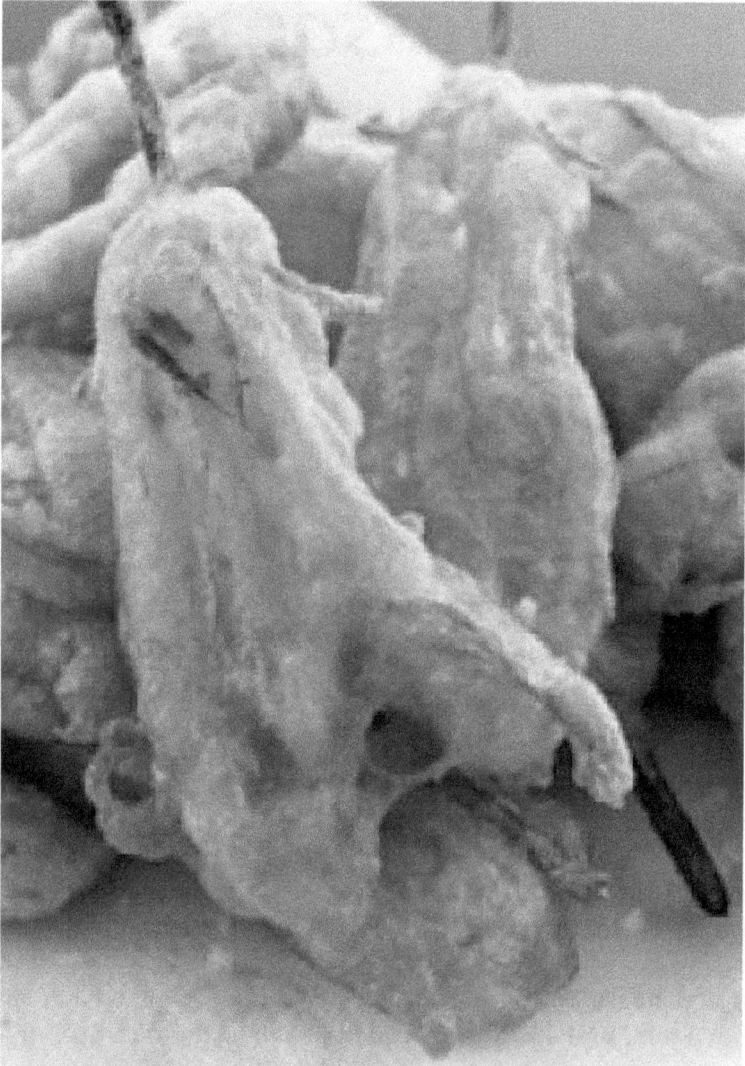

Notting Hill Publishing, London, UK © 2014

Fried Rice Balls (Arancini di Riso)

Fun and delicious, fried rice balls (Arancini di Riso) make great snacks and hors d'oeuvres. A few steps are involved but, the result is a tasty treat nearly everyone will love.

Ingredients

Vegetable oil
2 large eggs, beaten to blend
2 cups Risotto (follow recipe below)
1/2 cup grated Parmesan
1 1/2 cups dried Italian-style bread crumbs
2 ounces mozzarella, cut into 1/2-inch cubes
Salt

Risotto:
8 cups canned chicken broth (low sodium broth recommended)
1/4 cup butter
2 tablespoons olive oil
2 cups finely chopped onions
2 garlic cloves, minced
1 1/2 cups Arborio rice or short-grain white rice
2/3 cup dry white wine
2/3 cup grated Parmesan
Salt and freshly ground black pepper (to taste)

Notting Hill Publishing, London, UK © 2014

Directions to Prepare Risotto

You cannot rush Risotto, if you do, you'll end up with uncooked rice, and, the recipe for fried rice balls will fail miserably!

Begin by warming, but, not boiling your broth in a medium pot or pan.

Then, melt the butter in a separate heavy large pan over medium heat. Add olive oil. Add the onions and saute until tender, about 8 minutes. Add the garlic. Allow garlic to cook about 1 minute (do not brown. Browning garlic makes it bitter.) Now, stir in the rice and let it toast for 2 minutes. Add the wine and, cook until the liquid is absorbed, stirring often, about 2 minutes. Next, add 1 cup of hot broth at a time; simmer over medium-low heat until the liquid is absorbed (stirring often.) Repeat until all liquid is used and has absorbed into the rice. Mix in the Parmesan and still well. Season with salt and pepper, to taste.

Tip: Contrary to popular believe there is no cream or milk used in Risotto. The creamy texture comes from the slow sauté and cooking process.

Prepare and Fry the Rice Balls:

Pour enough oil in a heavy large pan to reach the depth of 3 inches. Heat the oil over medium heat.

In the meantime, mix the eggs, risotto, Parmesan, and 1/2 cup of the bread crumbs in a large bowl to combine. Place the remaining breadcrumbs in a medium bowl. Using about 2 tablespoons (more to make larger balls) of the risotto mixture for each, and, use your hands to roll into balls. Next, insert 1 cube of mozzarella into the center of each ball. Roll the balls in the bread crumbs to coat.

Working in batches, add the rice balls to the hot oil and cook until brown and heated through, turning them so each side cooks and becomes golden brown. Using a slotted spoon, transfer the rice balls to paper towels to drain. Season with salt. Let rest 2 minutes. Serve hot.

Tip: Once you have this recipe master, you can make hundreds of variations, simply by changing the type of risotto you prepare. Experiment and create one and make it your own!

Notting Hill Publishing, London, UK © 2014

Pastas, Pizza, Polenta, Sauces & Sides

Creamy Polenta

Polenta is far more common in Northern Italy, often taking the place of pasta. (Often said to be similar to American grits.)

Ingredients

4 cups water, plus more as needed
4 cups milk, plus more as needed
3 tablespoons butter
2 teaspoons salt
2 cups polenta
1/2 cup sour cream
1/3 cup Parmigiano-Reggiano (Parmesan cheese)

Directions

In a large saucepan, bring the water, milk and butter to a boil. Then add 2 teaspoons of salt to the water and whisk in the polenta. Whisk constantly for at least 5 minutes to prevent lumps. Lower heat, and, simmer for 45 minutes. Keep pot partially covered and stir the polenta every few minutes, until it is thick, smooth, and creamy. Add the sour cream and Parmesan cheese. Check and adjust consistency by adding milk (1 tablespoon at a time) to the polenta. Serve immediately.

Creamy Polenta

Pizza Margherita

There are few people in the world who don't enjoy a good pizza, and, in the United States there are all types of variations on this Neapolitan favorite. The recipe below is for the classic Pizza Margherita which is simply the crust, tomato sauce (marinara sauce), basil and mozzarella cheese. (If you plan on "ruining" this pizza with pineapple or other toppings that belong elsewhere please don't ever tell me!!)

And, don't be intimidated by attempting to make pizza dough at home. It's unbelievably easy!

Ingredients

For dough:

- 3 1/2 cups bread flour**
- 1 teaspoon sugar
- 1 envelope instant dry yeast
- 2 teaspoons salt
- 1 1/2 cups warm water
- 2 tablespoons olive oil, plus 2 teaspoons

**Bread flour will give you a crisp crust. If you can't find bread flour, you can substitute it with all-purpose flour which will produce a chewier crust.

Directions for Pizza Dough

Combine the bread flour, sugar, yeast and kosher salt in the bowl of a stand mixer and combine. Add the water and 2 tablespoons of the oil while the mixer is going, and, allow to mix until the dough forms into a ball.

Sticky dough?

If the dough is sticky, add additional flour, 1 tablespoon at a time, until the dough comes together in a solid ball.

Dough too dry?

If the dough is too dry, add additional water, 1 tablespoon at a time until a solid ball is formed.

Once the ball of dough is formed, grease a large bowl with the remaining 2 teaspoons olive oil, add the dough, cover the bowl with plastic wrap and put it in a warm area to let it double in size.

(This takes about 1 hour.)

Once the dough has doubled in size, place the dough on a lightly floured surface and divide it into 2 equal pieces. Cover each with a clean kitchen towel or plastic wrap and let them rest for 10 minutes.

Now you're ready to make pizza!

Kneading Pizza Dough/arinas74

Forming Your Pizza With The Dough

Do not punch down. Lightly dust the dough with flour, then transfer to a parchment-lined pizza peel or large baking sheet. Pat out dough evenly with your fingers and stretch into a 14-inch round, re-flouring fingers if necessary. Don't worry if your pizza isn't perfectly round and don't attempt the pizzeria toss unless you've done it before now!

For topping:

- Marinara sauce (see page)
- 4 basil leaves plus more for sprinkling
- 6 ounces fresh mozzarella, cut into 1/4-inch-thick slices
- Equipment: a pizza stone

Heat pizza stone while dough rises:
At least 45 minutes before baking pizza, put stone on oven rack in lower third of electric oven (or on floor of gas oven) and preheat oven to 500°F.

Assemble pizza:
Spread sauce over dough, leaving a 1-inch border (there may be some sauce left over). Arrange cheese on top, leaving a 2- to 3-inch border.

Slide pizza onto your pizza stone. Bake until dough is crisp and browned and cheese is golden and bubbling in spots, 13 to 16 minutes. Remove from oven, and, transfer pizza to a cutting board. Cool 5 minutes. Sprinkle with some basil leaves before slicing.

Enjoy!

Photo by Robert Bonhomme

Pizzeria e Friggitoria Di Matteo, Naples, Italy

47

Lemon Pasta

A friend of mine was on a long term work assignment in London, and, he came across a lemon pasta that he absolutely loved. He spent months trying to figure out the right combination of ingredients to make lemon pasta, but, something was always off. That's when he turned to me and asked me to experiment to see if I could come up with a good recipe for homemade Lemon Pasta.

It should be noted this is actual pasta with lemon flavor, and, not a lemon sauce for pasta.

Recommended: Use Lemon Pasta with Shrimp Scampi. Delicious!

Ingredients

- 1½ cups of all purpose flour
- ¼ cup of semolina flour*
- 1 tsp salt
- 2 – 3 tablespoons of fresh lemon juice**
- 2 Large Eggs
- 3 teaspoons lemon zest***

Semolina flour is an important part of the recipe. It is available in most major supermarkets and Italian specialty stores.

**Start with 2 tablespoons of lemon juice. If the pasta dough is too dry, use another tablespoon of lemon juice instead of water to bring it to the right consistency.

***When zesting your lemons make sure not to dig into the white part (that is between the skin and the flesh of the fruit. A rasp zester usually works best.)

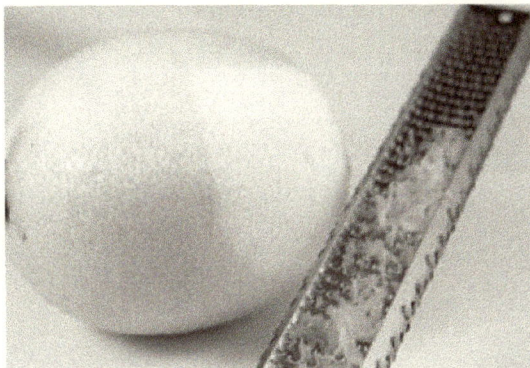

Photo by Robert Bonhomme

Preparation

On a large, clean surface (such as a counter-top – ideally a marble or granite counter-top) combine the all purpose flower and semolina flour with the salt.   Mix the ingredients together, and, form a well. (The middle should be much lower than the sides. See photo.)

Proceed to place all the wet ingredients (the two large eggs, the lemon juice, and the lemon zest) in a bowl and mix together. *Remember to keep the extra tablespoon of lemon on the side in case you need to add it to make the pasta to bring it to the correct consistency.*

In the center of the well you created with the flour mixture begin to slowly add your wet ingredients, and, begin to mix *(your hands work best so put down that fork or spoon. And, no, do NOT place it in your food processor to mix!)* Work from the inside out (in other words, bring the flour that is closest to the wet ingredients into the well first, leaving the outer flour mixture for later until the entire mixture is combined and a ball has been formed.)

49

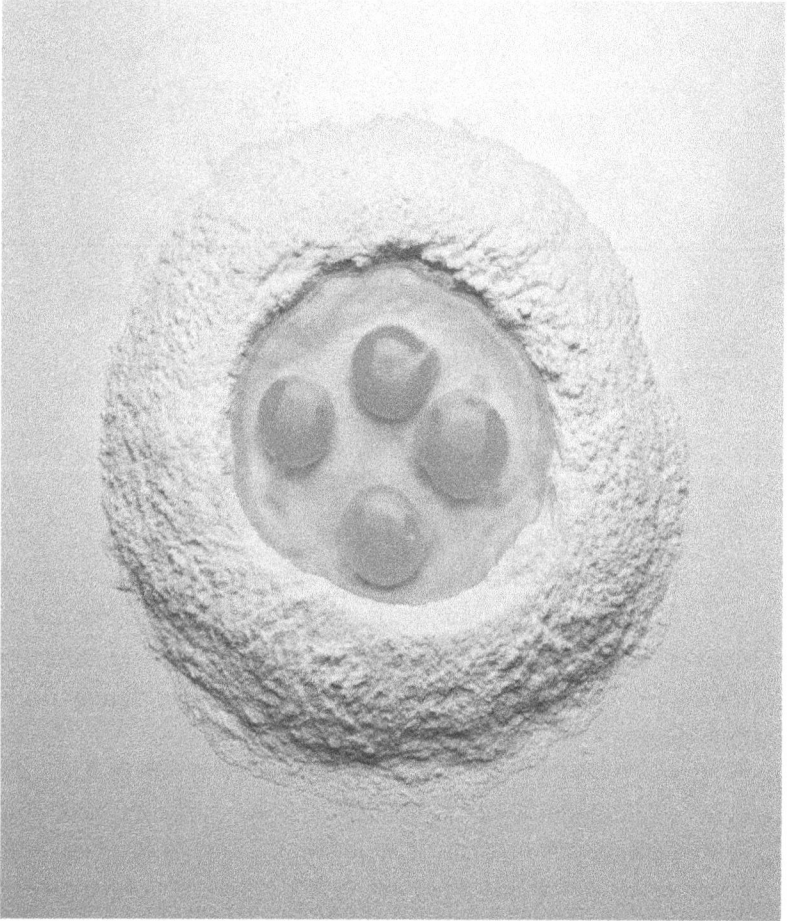

If the dough feels sticky, add extra semolina flour (one teaspoon at a time.) If the dough isn't sticky enough add the extra lemon juice. (If it still isn't the right consistency then slowly add a few drops of water.)

The consistency you are seeking is a semi-sticky dough. The best "test" for consistency is if the dough is *slightly* resistant and *slightly* sticks to the counter surface. It should not be sticking to your hands at all.

The next step is to knead the dough.

Before beginning to knead, place all purpose flour on the counter-top, and, spread out a very thin layer of flour. Place your ball of dough in it, and, begin the kneading process with your hands. Keep kneading the dough for 15 minutes. Again, do NOT use a food processor for kneading, it will not work! Pasta dough requires good, old-fashion muscle power!

Kneading Technique for Fresh Pasta

Take the dough and form it into a ball. Now, using the heal (palm) of your hand start rolling the dough away from you.

Next, fold the dough over on to itself, turn it about ¼ to the right, and, repeat the kneading as described above.

Continue kneading for 15 minutes.

After 15 minutes of kneading (and yes, your arms are going to feel like lead at this point) place the dough in a bowl and cover with plastic wrap. Place the dough somewhere it can rest for at least one hour. If you refrigerate the dough remember to allow time for the dough to come back to room temperature before proceeding to the next step.

Shaping and Cutting Fresh Pasta

Take your rested dough, and, cut into four, equal sized pieces. (Keep the dough you aren't using covered with a kitchen towel.) Dust your work area on your counter very lightly with flours, and, place the first section of dough on it. With a rolling pin, take the first section of dough, and, roll out until you have a rectangle shape approximately

10 inches by 20 inches. (The dough should be almost paper thin when you are done.)

With a very sharp knife create strips of pasta that are roughly 10 inches long and ½ inch wide to make fettuccini noodles or 10 inches long and ¼ wide for linguini noodles.

(If you are using a pasta machine, follow the directions that came with your specific machine.)

Once the noodles are created, allow them to dry for at least 20 minutes before cooking.

Cooking Fresh Pasta

Fresh pasta cooks super fast, and, you can't leave it unattended. Begin by bring a large pot of water to a boil (approximately 6 quarts of water for every pound of pasta) Once the water is at a rolling boil, add 1 tablespoon of salt (the salt helps flavor the pasta) Cook pasta 2 to 4 minutes for al dente (this mean "to the tooth") and it should be firm, but, not hard, and, not at all mushy.

Enjoy!

Nonna's (Grandma's) Wooden Spoon

Did you ever notice that every Italian Grandma (Nonna) in the world seems to own a wooden spoon, and, that she only uses a wooden spoon when making tomato sauce (gravy)? Turns out Grandma was pretty smart! Here's why...

It's a matter of chemistry. Tomatoes are an acid food, and, acid foods and metal spoons often react together; using a metal spoon while making tomato sauce can result in a "melt taste". Makes sense, right? Enter, Grandma's wooden spoon! She was right all along!

oto by Robert Bonhomme

Wooden Spoon Care

Caring for a wood spoon isn't difficult, and, it uses the same cleaning technique as your wood cutting board. Never put it in the dishwasher. Always hand wash with a mild detergent and warm water. Treat (or rub) the spoon at least two times a year with a food grade mineral oil to keep it from drying out. (If you use the spoon frequently then it is recommended you treat the spoon with mineral oil at least once a month.) The oil treatment also helps the wood stay strong and helps prevent bacteria and mold from attaching itself and growing. Allow wooden spoons to dry completely after an oil treatment before using.

Notting Hill Publishing, London, UK © 2014

Marinara Sauce

1/2 cup extra-virgin olive oil

2 small onions, finely chopped

2 garlic cloves, finely chopped

1/2 teaspoon sea salt, plus more to taste

1/2 teaspoon freshly ground black pepper, plus more to taste

2 (32 ounce) cans whole tomatoes

1 teaspoon, pre-mixed Italian seasoning (found in the spice aisle of your supermarket)

Directions:

Open the cans of tomatoes, and, crush using a potato masher or place in a blender for smoother sauce.

In a large pot, heat the oil over a medium-high flame. Add the onions and garlic and saute until the onions are translucent, about 10 minutes. Add salt and pepper. Add the tomatoes and Italian seasoning, and simmer uncovered over low heat about 1 hour. Season the sauce with more salt and pepper to taste.

Photo by Robert Bonhomme

Sunday Sauce (Gravy)

This recipe is not to be rushed, and, in fact, "Sunday Sauce" should actually be made on Friday or Saturday if you're planning to use it on Sunday. Two things are critical in helping this recipe turn out right – the first, is do NOT skimp on ingredients. If you really can't afford something, then, yes, of course, substitute, but, keep in mind that lower grade ingredients will produce a lower grade sauce; the second item to success is time. Never, ever rush the cooking process or serve this sauce the same day. Aging it overnight will allow the ingredients to really mix and marry. (That's one of the reasons the food you bring home from an Italian restaurant always tastes better the next day!)

Ingredients

- 2 pounds piece lean beef, veal and pork meat mixture (sometimes referred to meatloaf mixture. It can be found in most grocery stores or ask your butcher to mix it for you.) This mixture will be used to make meatballs.
- 1 pound hot or sweet Italian sausage (it's just a matter of personal preference, and, yes, you may use both if you wish. It is also acceptable to use other sausages such as turkey or veal, but, the taste of the sauce may change slightly due to this variation.)
- 1 pound chuck (that is cubed into 1" pieces)
- 1/2 cup olive oil
- 4 to 6 garlic cloves, peeled (adjust to taste)
- 3 tablespoons tomato paste
- 3 Tablespoons Parmigiano Reggiano** (if you cannot afford the pricey Parmigiano Reggiano, use a lower grade parmesan cheese)
- 3 (35-ounce) cans San Marzano plum tomatoes *

- 1 can tomato sauce (this is **NOT** pre-made jar sauce, but, rather tomato sauce in a can)
- Salt and pepper

*** Parmigiano Reggiano is a brand, not a type of parmesan cheese*

*San Marzano tomatoes are grown just outside Naples, Italy, near Mount Vesuvius. It is due to the volcanic soil in the region that these specific tomatoes have become known as the "best" plum tomatoes in the world. Many companies have jumped on the San Marzano tomatoes band wagon, and, claim to be San Marzano tomatoes. To insure you have authentic San Marzano tomatoes, that are imported tomatoes from the Campania region in Italy, simply check the label on the can. Again, you may use a less expensive canned tomato, but, the results will not be the same.

Instructions

To begin chop or dice the garlic very finely, set aside. In the meantime, in a large frying pan, place your sausage into the pan with ½ cup of water, and, place on high heat. Allow the water to evaporate, and, then brown the sausage in it's own fat. If there isn't enough fat, add 1 tablespoon of high quality olive oil to brown.

Then, in a large, deep pot, heat oil over medium heat. Add the garlic and toss to coat with oil. Add chuck and cook meat a few pieces at a time until nicely browned on all sides – about five minutes per batch. Remove meat from pan and set aside. If you do not care for garlic in the sauce itself, now is the time to remove and discard the garlic cloves. Combine tomato paste and water and stir into oil. Stirring constantly, cook for 2 to 3 minutes. Add the tomatoes, raise heat, and bring to a boil. Using a tomato can, measure 1 can of cold water, add to pan, and return to a boil. Return beef to the sauce, and add salt and pepper, to taste. Bring to a boil and allow to boil for 5 minutes. Lower heat and partially cover pan. Cook for approximately 2 hours stirring occasionally until meat is almost falling apart and sauce is thick. One hour before sauce is ready, add the beef or pork braciola and sausage. Add the meatballs at the same time.

Storing The Sauce (Gravy)

Be sure to properly store your sauce until you wish to use it. The best way to store the sauce is to place it in several shallow containers with air tight lids for quick cooling and place them in your refrigerator (the sauce should reach 40 °F or below within two hours.) This method complies with the government recommended standards for food handling and storage.

Notting Hill Publishing, London, UK © 2014

Spaghetti alla Carbonara

While it sounds easy, Carbonara is actually one of the most difficult Italian dishes to prepare. It takes practice and timing to learn how to add the egg without scrambling it. The key to success is practice!

Ingredients

1 pound dry spaghetti
2 tablespoons extra-virgin olive oil
4 ounces pancetta or slab bacon, cubed or sliced into small strips
4 garlic cloves, finely chopped
2 large eggs
1 cup freshly grated Parmigiano-Reggiano (parmesan cheese), plus more for serving
Freshly ground black pepper
1 handful fresh flat-leaf parsley, chopped

Directions

Prepare the sauce while the pasta is cooking to ensure that the spaghetti will be hot and ready when the sauce is finished; it is very important that the pasta is hot when adding the egg mixture, so that the heat of the pasta cooks the raw eggs in the sauce. (Learning how to add the egg without scrambling it can be a challenge, don't give up after your first attempt. You will need practice to get it right.)

Bring a large pot of salted water to a boil, add the pasta and cook for 8 to 10 minutes or until tender yet firm (as they say in Italian "al dente"meaning to the tooth.) Drain the pasta well, reserving 1/2 cup of the starchy cooking water to use in the sauce if you wish.

Meanwhile, heat the olive oil in a deep skillet over medium flame. Add the pancetta and saute for about 3 minutes, until the bacon is crisp and the fat is rendered. Toss the garlic into the fat and saute for less than 1 minute to soften.   Remove garlic.

Add the hot, drained spaghetti to the pan and toss for 2 minutes to coat the strands in the bacon fat.

Beat the eggs and Parmesan together in a mixing bowl, stirring well to prevent lumps. (Make in advance while the pasta is cooking and have the "sauce" ready for the next step.)

Remove the pan from the heat and pour the egg/cheese mixture on the pasta, whisking quickly until the eggs thicken, but do not scramble (this is done off the heat to ensure this does not happen.)

Thin out the sauce with a bit of the reserved pasta water, until it reaches desired consistency. Season the carbonara with several turns of freshly ground black pepper and taste for salt. Mound the spaghetti carbonara into warm serving bowls and garnish with chopped parsley. Pass more cheese around the table. Serve immediately.

Linguine with

White Clam Sauce

Ingredients

Extra-virgin olive oil **
9 cloves garlic, smashed
5 dozen littleneck clams, scrubbed under cold running water
1 cup white wine
1/2 cup water
1 large pinch crushed red pepper flakes
1 pound linguine
2 tablespoons butter
2 tablespoons chopped Italian parsley leaves
2 tablespoons chopped oregano leaves
1 cup grated Parmigiano-Reggiano, optional, plus shavings for garnish
Salt

**Purchase the best quality olive oil you can afford, it DOES make a difference!

Directions

In a large pan, add olive oil and about half the garlic cloves. Bring the pan to a medium- high heat and cook until the garlic becomes golden. When the garlic is golden remove it and discard. Do not allow garlic to brown or your sauce will be bitter.

Now, put 3 1/2 dozen clams in the pan with the wine and 1/2 cup of water. Cover the pan and bring it to a boil over medium heat. Cover

and cook until the clams open, about 10 minutes. Remove the clams from the pan and reduce the liquid by half. Let the clams cool slightly, then remove them from the shells and reserve. If a clam has failed to open, discard it, it is not safe to eat. Pour the cooking liquid into a measuring cup., and, use a triple layered cheese cloth to strain the liquid to help remove sand and grit. Strain the liquid at least twice using clean cheese cloth each time. *Otherwise – yuck! Who wants to eat sand and grit?*

Bring a large pot of well salted water to a boil over medium heat.

Coat the same pan again with olive oil and add the remaining garlic cloves and a large pinch of crushed pepper flakes. Bring the pan to a medium-high heat and cook until the garlic becomes golden. When the garlic is golden, remove it and discard, *(again, browning garlic makes it bitter, and, in turn your sauce will be bitter.)* Add the remaining raw clams and reserved clam cooking liquid to the pan. Cover and cook until the clams open. *If a clam fails to open, discard it, it is not safe to eat.*

While the clams are cooking, drop the linguine into the salted boiling water and cook until the pasta is very "al dente" (follow directions on your pasta box for la dente.)

Remove the cooked clams in their shells from the pan and keep warm. Add the butter and cooked clams that have been removed from their shells back to the pan. Bring the liquid to a boil and toss in the cooked pasta and the herbs. Cook the pasta together with the sauce until the sauce clings to the pasta – about 1 minute. Turn off the heat and toss in the grated Parmigiano-Reggiano, and, if desired, finish with a sprinkling of extra virgin olive oil. Don't use much – a teaspoon or less will do!

Linguine with Red Clam Sauce

Red clam sauce is far less challenging to prepare than white clam sauce, but, it is just as delicious!

Ingredients

3 (6 ½ ounce) cans minced clams
1/4 cup extra-virgin olive oil
6 cloves garlic, minced
1/2 teaspoon red pepper flakes or more to taste
One 28-ounce can whole tomatoes packed in juice, drained, and chopped
1 pound dry spaghetti or linguini
10 fresh basil leaves, chopped
2 tablespoons finely chopped flat-leaf parsley
Salt
Black pepper

Directions

Drain the clams reserving 1/2 cup of their juice and set aside.

Heat the olive oil in a large pan over medium-low heat. Add the garlic and cook until translucent. Add the pepper flakes and cook for 30 seconds. Add the reserved clam juice and tomatoes, increase the heat and bring to a boil. Cover, and lower the heat to maintain a gentle simmer, cook for 15 minutes. Set aside.

Bring a large pot of water to a boil over high heat, salt generously. Cook the pasta until al dente, tender yet still slightly firm. During the last 5 minutes of cooking the pasta stir the clams, basil, and parsley into the sauce. Bring to a simmer and season with salt and pepper to taste. Drain the pasta and add to the sauce and toss to combine and serve immediately. See! Easy, right?

Meats & Fish

Shrimp Scampi

Ingredients

- 1 1/2 pound shrimp, shelled and deveined**
- Kosher salt and freshly ground black pepper
- 2 tablespoons unsalted butter
- 2 teaspoons minced garlic
- (Optional) pinch of red pepper flakes
- 1/4 cup dry white wine (Pinot Grigio works very well)*
- 1 tablespoon freshly squeezed lemon juice
- 2 teaspoons finely chopped flat-leaf parsley leaves
- 1/4 teaspoon grated lemon zest

***Large shrimp (meaning 24 to 30 count) work best for this recipe. Jumbo shrimp may be substituted.*

** Pinot Grigio is recommended. Some recipes call for white vermouth, and, it can be used in this recipe, however, if you're unaccustomed to the flavor of vermouth, you may find it over-powering as the flavor is very strong. If you aren't certain stick with the Pinot Grigio or your favorite dry white wine.*

Instructions

Begin by rising the shrimp thoroughly with cold water then proceed to shell, and, devein them. Rise again and squeeze the juice of 1 lemon over them. Allow them to absorb the lemon juice for 5 minutes. Pat with a paper towel and allow to dry completely. Arrange the shrimp so they lay flat and are evenly spaced.

Heat a large skillet over medium heat. Season the shrimp with salt and pepper (before putting them in the skillet.)

Add the butter to the skillet. Allow the butter to melt, but, do not brown it. Add in your garlic and red pepper flakes.

Now add the shrimp. Make sure the shrimp are in a single layer otherwise they will not cook properly. If necessary, make the shrimp in batches.

Cook the shrimp for approximately 2 minutes. Then flip and cook the other side for two minutes. Remove the shrimp, and, reduce the heat. Add your white wine, lemon and lemon zest. Boil until slightly thickened (about 30 seconds.)

Place the shrimp back in the skillet to quickly warm (about 30 seconds.) Remove shrimp to serving platter or dishes, and, pour the sauce over the shrimp. Garnish with parsley. Serve immediately.

How To Devein Shrimp

Start by pulling off the head (if it is still attached) and then proceed to pull off the outer shell. It is your choice to leave the tail on or tail it off. For eating purposes it is easier to take the tail out now.

Once you have removed the shell, head and optional tail proceed to cut down the back of the shrimp using a small paring knife. (About ¼ inch deep.)

Most times you will see a dark vein, this should be removed. Some people leave it in, but, for presentation purposes and eating purposes, it is better to remove it. (Otherwise, the shrimp will have a very gritty, dirty taste.)   If you do not see the dark vein, rinse the entire shrimp and place in a bowl of ice water. Repeat until all your shrimp are pealed and deveined.

You can also opt to have your seafood store clean the shrimp for you, it will cost more, but, it also saves time.

Baccalà

(Zuppa di Baccala)

Have you ever gone into an Italian specialty store or a grocery store around the holidays, and, went to the fish counter and saw something that looked like you could shingle your house with it? That's Baccalà!

Baccalà is salted cod fish, and, it's origins are at least 500 years old. And, it is a very common product in Italian cooking – especially at Christmas time. There are many ways to prepare Baccalà, and, Zuppa di Baccala is merely one of them.

Note: Since the fish is already heavily salted, no further salt is required or recommended for this dish.

Ingredients

4 pounds dried salt cod, cut into 3-inch pieces, soaked
8 to 10 all-purpose potatoes, peeled and quartered
1 cup extra virgin olive oil
1 bunch celery, trimmed, well washed, and cut into 3-inch pieces
1 large onion, chopped
2 cups pitted Gaeta olives
4 (28-ounce) cans San Marzano plum tomatoes
12 cups chicken broth

Directions

Soak the cod in cold water to cover in a cool spot or refrigerator for at least 24 hours (48 hours is better) and change the water frequently.

To prepare:
Begin by placing the potatoes in cold water to cover in a large pot. Bring to a boil over high heat and cook for about 15 minutes or until potatoes are folk soft. Drain.

Heat the olive oil in a large, heavy bottomed casserole or pot over medium heat. Add the celery and saute for about 5 minutes, then add the onion and saute until vegetables begin to get soft. Add the olives and saute for an additional minute. Stir in the tomatoes and their juice. Bring to a boil. Lower heat and simmer for 10 minutes.

Stir in the chicken broth and return to simmer.

Stir in the cooked potatoes and the soaked baccala and simmer for about 10 minutes or until the baccala flakes when poked with a fork. Serve hot.

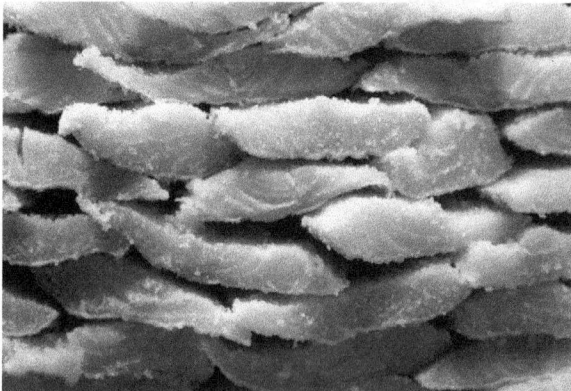

Salt cured cod is known as Baccalà in Italian

Meatballs

To Fry or Not To Fry (That is the Question)

Some people prefer not to fry their meatballs, however, every precaution must be taken if this step is skipped because you are adding raw meat into your sauce. Frying prior to adding to sauce is highly recommended.

Ingredients

- 1 pound ground lean beef
- 1/2 pound ground veal
- 1/2 pound ground pork
- 2 eggs
- 1/2 cup freshly grated Pecorino Romano
- 1/2 cup Parmigiano Reggiano
- 1 1/2 tablespoons chopped Italian parsley
- Salt and pepper (both to taste)
- 2 cups bread crumbs

Directions

In a large bowl combine cheeses, parsley, salt, pepper, and, breadcrumbs together. After mixing the dry ingredients together, add the eggs, and, again mix until thoroughly combined. Now add all three meats.

Using your hand, mix everything together until very well blended. The mixture should hold together, and, should be on the dry side without being crumbly. Many recipes call for milk or water, however, this tends to make a rather mushy meatball. This recipe will produce firmer meatballs.

Once you have the meatball mixture blended, begin forming your meatballs. Take the meat mixture, and, roll into balls using your hands. Meatballs should be about 1.5 inches diameter. Set aside until all are complete.

If you do not wish to fry your meatballs (NOT RECOMMENDED), you can now place them in your Sunday Sauce, and, cook for at least 1.5 hours over medium heat.

If you fry your meatballs (recommended), in a large fry pan, add olive oil until it is roughly half way up the side of the pan. Bring to high heat, and, begin frying your meatballs in small batches. Allow meatballs to brown but not burn on each side (about 5 minutes total cooking time in the oil). Remove meatball and place on plate covered with paper towels to absorb excess grease. Repeat until all meatballs have been fried. Now add your fried meatballs to your Sunday Sauce, and, cook another 45 minutes over medium heat. Serve with pasta or by themselves.

Braciole

Like sauce (or gravy) every Italian family has their own version of braciole, and, there are too many variations to count! The basic idea is to take a piece of steak (although some people use chicken or pork), and, fill it with delicious things, roll it up, and, then slow cook it for hours resulting in a wonderful treat. _Also like making sauce/gravy, the cooking of braciole cannot be rushed. Traditionally, cheaper cuts of meat are used, and, usually require hours of cooking to make them folk tender._

Ingredients

- 1/2 cup dried Italian-style bread crumbs
- 2 garlic cloves, finely minced
- 2/3 cup grated Pecorino Romano
- (Optional) 1/3 cup grated provolone (mozzarella may be substituted)
- (Optional) 1/2 cup pine nuts, toasted
- (Optional) 1/2 cup raisins, soaked in warm water to rehydrate then drained
- (Optional) 1 hard boiled egg, chopped
- 2 tablespoons chopped fresh Italian parsley leaves
- 4 tablespoons olive oil
- Salt and freshly ground black pepper
- 1 (1 1/2-pound) flank steak
- 1 cup dry white wine
- 3 1/4 cups Sunday Sauce (page) or Marinara Sauce (page)

The optional ingredients are just that – optional. It is just a matter of personal preferences, you may select all or merely what appeals to you from the optional ingredients.

Photo by Robert Bonhomme

Notting Hill Publishing, London, UK © 2014

Instructions

Stir the bread crumbs, garlic, Pecorino Romano, and optional provolone (or mozzarella), pine nuts, raisins, and, chopped egg in a medium bowl to blend. Stir in 2 tablespoons of the oil. Season mixture with salt and pepper and set aside.

Take your flank steak, and, pound it with a meat tenderizer until flat. Cut into equal pieces (1.5 steak should produce between 6 to 10 individual cutlets. Size is just a matter of personal preference.)

Take the pieces of the pounded <u>flank steak</u> and place on your work surface. Sprinkle the bread crumb mixture evenly over the steak to cover the top evenly. Starting at 1 short end, roll up the steak as for a <u>jelly roll</u> to enclose the filling completely. Using butcher's twine, tie the steak roll to secure. Sprinkle the braciole with salt and pepper. Repeat until each individual braciole done.

Preheat the oven to 350 degrees F.

Heat the remaining 2 tablespoons of oil in a heavy large ovenproof skillet over medium heat. Add the braciole and cook until browned on all sides, about 8 minutes. Add the wine to the pan (this will deglaze the pan) and then bring the wine to a boil. Stir in the Sunday Sauce (or marinara sauce.) Cover the pan loosely with foil and bake until the meat is tender, turning the braciole and basting with the sauce every 30 minutes. After 1 hour, uncover and continue baking until the meat is tender, about 30 minutes longer. The total cooking time should be about 1 1/2 hours.

Be sure to remove all string from each braciole before serving. Place on large serving plate, and, top with the sauce remaining on the pan. It may also be served over pasta.

Steak Florentine

As you proceed North in Italy, fish becomes less common and meat becomes a staple in both homes and restaurants. Steak Florentine is a favorite for locals and visitors alike!

Ingredients:

- 2 T-bone or porterhouse steaks, each about 1 3/4 lb. and 1 1/2 inches thick
- Salt and freshly ground pepper (to taste)
- 2 cups tender, young arugula leaves
- Parmigiano-Reggiano parmesan cheese wedge (cut into thin shavings)
- Extra-virgin olive oil for drizzling

Directions:

Prepare a medium-hot fire in a grill and let burn until the coals are covered with white ash. This method is less likely to flare up during cooking.

Using tongs place the steaks on the grill, about 5 inches above the coals. Grill the first side until it is well browned, 5 to 7 minutes. Turn the steaks over, and, cook for another 5 to 7. Remove from grill and season with salt and pepper to taste immediately.

Transfer the steaks to a carving board and cut across the grain into 1/2-inch slices . Arrange the slices on a serving platter and top with any juices accumulated on the carving board. Place the arugula and Parmigiano-Reggiano (parmesan cheese) on top, drizzle with olive oil and serve immediately.

Roman Style Lamb Chops

Ingredients:

- 8 to 12 lamb chops (about 1.5 inches thick each)
- 3 fresh bay leaves (optional)
- 3 sage leaves (optional)
- 1 sprig fresh rosemary
- A few juniper berries
- Sea Salt
- Black peppercorns
- 1/2 glass dry white wine
- 6 tablespoons Extra Virgin Olive Oil
- 2 lemons, cut into wedges

Directions:

Layer the lamb chops in a large container.

Combine all the spices you are using together, crush, and, mix with wine and olive oil to make a marinade. Pour the mixture over the lamb in the container and allow to marinate overnight.

Cooking Times

- Medium-rare (145°F) - 5 Minutes
- Medium (160°F) – 8 Minutes
- Well Done (170°F) - 10 minutes

Lamb cooks very fast, and, may be served medium rare, medium or well done. Some people prefer it rare, and, unlike pork it is safe to serve rare lamb.

Place chops on grill, and, follow suggested timing found above.

Desserts and Sweets

Photo by Robert Bonhomme

Notting Hill Publishing, London, UK © 2014

Cannoli

No, you aren't misreading, there really IS wine in the shells!

Shells:

2 cups all-purpose flour

1 tablespoon granulated sugar

1/4 teaspoon salt

1 tablespoon plus 2 teaspoons unsalted butter, cut into small pieces

1 egg yolk

1/2 cup dry white wine (Marsala wine can also be used)

Filling:

2 cups ricotta cheese, preferably whole milk

3/4 cup powdered sugar

1 teaspoon ground cinnamon

1/4 teaspoon allspice

1/4 cup heavy cream

1/4 cup small semisweet chocolate chips

1 lemon

1 quart canola oil, for frying

Flour, for rolling

1 egg, lightly beaten, for egg wash

Powdered sugar, for dusting

Directions

Tip: Drain ricotta cheese in a cheese cloth overnight to drain excess liquid off, otherwise, the filling will be watery. Place a colander into a large bowl, and, put down two layers of cheese cloth in the colander, place ricotta on top of cheese cloth. The bowl will catch the liquid as it drains. Place in refrigerator, drain overnight.

Shell Dough:

In a medium bowl, sift together the flour, sugar and salt. Mix the butter pieces into the flour with your fingers until the mixture becomes coarse (you'll want a "sandy" feel and look to it.) Add the egg yolk and the white wine and mix until dough becomes smooth. Place the dough in the center of a long piece of plastic wrap and cover loosely around the mixture, and, refrigerate while you prepare the filling.

Filling:

In a medium bowl, whisk the ricotta (that was drained overnight) until smooth. Add the powdered sugar, cinnamon and allspice, and, blend together. In a separate bowl beat the heavy cream until stiff. Once done, gently fold the cream into the ricotta mixture. Stir in the chocolate chips. Lightly zest the exterior of the lemon and stir it into the ricotta. Refrigerate for at least one hour.

To roll and fry the shells:

In a heavy bottom pan, heat 1 cup of vegetable or canola oil to 360 degrees F. In the meantime, sift an even layer of flour on a flat surface. Flour a rolling pin. Roll the shell dough until it is very thin (about 1/8-inch thick).

Use any glass or small bowl that has a 3-to-4-inch diameter. Using a very sharp knife, cut rounds by tracing around the glass until it is a completely cut circle.

Wrap each circle around a cannoli mold. If you don't have a cannoli mold, you can make your own mold by wrapping a 1 ¼ inch dowel with aluminum foil.

Homemade Cannoli Mold Instructions

1. *Fold the aluminum foil in half with the dull side out.*
2. *Roll it tightly around the dowel.*
3. *Slid off and make a few more. Repeat until you feel you have made enough*

Once you have a mold – either store bought or homemade. Wrap your dough circles around the mold, and, use egg wash on the edge of each round to seal the shell. *Hint: Flare the edges out slightly from the mold. Flaring allows the oil to penetrate the shells as they fry.*

Now, using a pair of tongs to hold the edge of the mold as you submerge and fry the shell in the oil until crispy, about 2 to 3 minutes. Remove from the oil, and holding the mold in one had with your tongs, gently grip the shell in your other hand with a kitchen towel and carefully slide it off the mold. Set on paper towels to cool and drain off excess oil.

To fill the cannoli shells:

Just before serving, use a pastry bag without a tip to pipe the ricotta into the cannoli molds. If you don't have a pastry bag, a small spoon will work.

Fill the cannoli shells from both ends so the cream runs through the whole shell. If you're using a spoon to fill the fill, start inside and work outward.

Dust with powdered sugar. Powdered sugar gives that little extra sweetness and added texture to the exterior. Keep in the refrigerator until ready to serve.

Tip: Do not fill shells until you're ready to serve, otherwise, they will be soggy!

Granita

Ever have an Italian Ice? Well, it's based on Granita!   And, it's a very easy dessert, and, wonderful summer-time treat! In some restaurants in Italy, granitas are served as a palate cleanser between courses (just like sorbet is used in the United States for this same purpose); and, the best part is this is a super easy recipe!

- 1 cup of filtered water
- 1/3 to 1/2 cup of sugar
- 1/2 cup of additional flavoring of your choice. Generally speaking, juices, fruit purees, and, coffee produce the best Granitas.

Begin by making a simple syrup. Combine the water and sugar in a saucepan and simmer on medium heat until the sugar dissolves.

Remove the pot from the heat. Add any solid flavoring agents such as your juices, fruit, coffee, etc., blend and then allow to cool for at least 30 minutes. Now pour the mixture into a flat-bottomed pan or glass dish. Then place the mixture in the freezer for 30 minutes. After 30 minutes, stir the mixture very thoroughly with a fork and allow it to freeze for another 30 minutes. Repeat this process every 30 minutes for four hours.(You're doing this to avoid creating one solid mass of ice.) Serve after 4 hours.

Spinge

(Italian Doughnuts)

These are super easy and super quick to make. Perfect with coffee or as snack.

Ingredients

- 1 cup water
- ½ stick butter
- 1 cup flour
- 1 teaspoon baking powder
- 1/4 teaspoon nutmeg
- 1/8 teaspoon salt
- 4 eggs
- 1 cup oil for frying**
- ½ cup confectioner's sugar
- ¼ cup cinnamon

Use a flavorless oil for frying such as vegetable oil or canola oil. Olive oil is too heavy and will make the doughnuts too greasy.

First, combine your confectioner's sugar and cinnamon together in a shallow pan or shallow container. Mix them together well (because you will be using this mixture to coat the doughnuts as they come out of the frying pan.) Set the confectioner's sugar and cinnamon combination aside for now.

In a small sauce pan or pot, combine the water and the butter and bring to a boil. In the meantime, with the exception of the sugar and cinnamon (which you already combined and set aside), combine your dry ingredients (flour, baking powder, nutmeg, and salt) and mix them together very well.

Once the water and butter is a boil, put the dry ingredients (flour, baking powder, nutmeg, and salt) in and remove from heat. Still vigorously to combine the ingredients, and, add 1 egg at a time and stir each well before adding the next egg. When done the dough will be sticky.

In another shallow pan heat your frying oil to 375 degrees. Using a small scoop or spoons create uniform balls of dough, and, drop into the oil. Fry until golden brown. Remove from oil and immediately place into the confectioner's sugar and cinnamon mix, roll around until completely coated.

Serve warm or cold. Enjoy!

Notting Hill Publishing, London, UK © 2014

Photo by Robert Bonhomme

Spinge (Italian Doughnuts)

Notting Hill Publishing, London, UK © 2014

Tiramsu

Like so many other Italian dishes, everyone has their own verison of Tiramsu. This is my version.

Ingredients

- **6 egg yolks**
- **1 cup sugar**
- **1¼ cup mascarpone cheese**
- **1¾ cup heavy whipping cream**
- **2 -7oz packages Italian Lady fingers**
- **1 cup cold espresso**
- **½ cup coffee flavored Liqueur (optional)**
- **1 tbsp cocoa for dusting**

Instructions

Combine egg yolks and sugar in the top of a double boiler, over boiling water. Reduce heat to low, and cook for about 10 minutes, stirring constantly. This is your sabayon, remove from the heat and whip yolks until thick and lemon colored.

Add Mascarpone to whipped yolks, beat until combined.

In a separate bowl, whip cream to stiff peaks.

Gently fold the whipped cream in the mascarpone sabayon mixture and set aside.

Mix the cold espresso with the coffee liquor and dip the lady fingers into the mixture just long enough to get them wet, do not soak them!

Arrange the lady fingers in the bottom of a 9 inch square baking dish (or container similarly sized)

Spoon half the mascarpone cream filling over the lady fingers.

Repeat process with another layer of lady fingers and cream.

Refrigerate 4 hours or overnight.

Dust with cocoa before serving

Rainbow Cookies

This recipe requires patience but it's well worth it!

Ingredients

- 7 ounces marzipan paste or almond paste
- 1 cup sugar
- 3 sticks unsalted butter, softened
- 4 large eggs, separated
- 1 teaspoon almond extract
- 2 cups sifted all-purpose flour (sift before measuring)
- 1/4 teaspoon salt
- 5 drops green food coloring, or to desired color
- 5 drops red food coloring, or to desired color
- 12-oz jar raspberry jam (preferably seedless)
- 6 ounces semisweet chocolate chips

Preparation

Preheat oven to 350°F and grease 3 (13- by 9-inch) metal baking pans. Line bottom of each with wax paper, letting it extend at 2 opposite ends, and grease paper otherwise, you'll have a mess on your hands trying to remove the cookies.

Break marzipan paste into small pieces and grind with sugar in food processor until no lumps remain.

Next take the marzipan and sugar mixture and place it into a large bowl and add the butter.

Next in a smaller, separate bowl add egg yolks and almond extract and blend together with an electric mixer.

Now combine the marzipan mixture with the egg yolk and almond mixture, and, using an electric beater, blend until flight and fluffy. Now, combine flour and salt, and, mix together, then add to this mixture, and, beat again (about 2 minutes.)

Next, whip the egg whites in another bowl with an electric mixer until they just hold stiff peaks. Add one third into batter to lighten slightly (batter will still be stiff). Fold in remaining whites thoroughly.

Next, divide dough into thirds (about 1 1/2 cups each). Stir green food coloring into one third and red food coloring into another, leaving one third plain. Spread each doughs into three different pans.

Bake in batches until just set and beginning to turn golden along edges (about 7 to 10 minutes total.) Run a knife along edges to loosen from pan, then while still hot, invert on to a large cooling rack, remove wax paper immediately and allow to cool completely.

Next, line a large shallow baking pan with wax paper and slide green layer into it. Spread half of jam evenly over green layer and carefully top with plain layer. Repeat for plain and pink layers. Cover with plastic wrap and weigh down, but, do not crush. Place in refrigerator and chill for at least 3 hours.

Now, melt chocolate in a double boiler or a metal bowl set over a pan of barely simmering water. Remove cake from refrigerator, remove plastic, and, proceed to cover the top with the melted chocolate. Use a spatula to cover top and sides. Let stand at room temperature until set, about 1 hour, and cut into small diamonds (12 rows crosswise and 12 diagonal rows). Serve. Wrap remaining pieces in plastic to prevent from drying out.

Special Occasions

Italy Loves A Celebration!

Italian Holidays and Religious Feast Days

Italy is predominately Roman Catholic, and, therefore, many religious feast days can be found on the Italian calendar, however, many of these days are regional, and, there are actually only a handful National holidays celebrated (where government offices, schools, and, banks are closed.)

NATIONAL HOLIDAYS AND FEAST DAYS (PUBLIC HOLIDAYS NATIONWIDE)

January

- **New Year's Day**
- **Epiphany**

April

- **Easter Day (Movable)**
- **Easter Monday (Movable)**
- **Liberation Day**

May

- **Labor Day / May Day**

June

- **Republic Day**

August

- **Assumption of Mary**

November

- **All Saints' Day**

December

- **Feast of the Immaculate Conception**
- **Christmas Day**
- **St. Stephen's Day**

ALL HOLIDAYS AND RELIGIOUS FEAST DAYS

January

Capodanno (New Year's Day)
Epifania/La Befana (Epiphany)
Giornata Nazionale della Bandiera (Flag Day)—celebrated principally in Reggio nell'Emilia

February

San Biagio (patron saint of Doues)
San Rinaldo (patron saint of Nocera Umbra)
Festa degli Innamorati (San Valentino)
Movable Date: Martedì Grasso (Mardi Gras / Fat Tuesday)—part of Carnevale
Movable Date: Mercoledì di Ceneri (Ash Wednesday)

March

La Festa della Donna
San Ilario and San Taziano (patron saints of Gorizia)
Festa del Papà (San Giuseppe)
San Proietto (patron saint of Randazzo)
Movable Date (can also occur in April): Domenica delle Palme (Palm Sunday)
Movable Date (can also occur in April): Venerdì Santo (Good Friday)
Movable Date (can also occur in April): Pasqua (Easter Sunday)
Monday after Easter (can also occur in April): Pasquetta, Lunedì di Pasqua (Easter Monday)

April

Pesce d'Aprile (April Fool's Day)
Festa della Liberazione (Liberation Day)
San Marco (patron saint of Venezia)

May

Festa del Lavoro (May Day)

June

Festa della Repubblica (Republic Day)
San Giovanni Battista (patron saint of Firenze)
San Pietro and San Paolo (patron saints of Roma)

July

San Paterniano (patron saint of Grottammare)
Santa Rosalia (patron saint of Palermo)

August

San Alessio (patron saint of Sant'Alessio in Aspromonte)
Ferragosto / Assunzione (Day of the Assumption)

September

San Gennaro (patron saint of Napoli)
San Maurizio (patron saint of Calasetta)

October

San Petronio (patron saint of Bologna)

November

Ognissanti (All Saints Day)
Il Giorno dei Morti (Day of the Dead)
San Giusto (patron saint of Trieste)
San Martino (patron saint of Foiano della Chiana)

December

San Nicola (patron saint of Bari)
Sant'Ambrogio (patron saint of Milano)
Immacolata Concezione (Immaculate Conception)
<u>Natale</u> (Christmas)
Santo Stefano (St. Stephen's Day)
San Silvestro (St. Silvester's Day)

Notting Hill Publishing, London, UK © 2014

www.ingramcontent.com/pod-product-compliance
Lightning Source LLC
LaVergne TN
LVHW011409080426
835511LV00005B/450